Forty-Two Poems

James Elroy Flecker

Contents

The Sentimentalist
Don Juan in Hell
The Ballad of Iskander

TO A POET
A THOUSAND YEARS HENCE

I who am dead a thousand years,
  And wrote this sweet archaic song,
Send you my words for messengers
  The way I shall not pass along.

I care not if you bridge the seas,
  Or ride secure the cruel sky,
Or build consummate palaces
  Of metal or of masonry.

But have you wine and music still,
  And statues and a bright-eyed love,
And foolish thoughts of good and ill,
  And prayers to them who sit above?

How shall we conquer? Like a wind
  That falls at eve our fancies blow,
And old Moeonides the blind
  Said it three thousand years ago.

O friend unseen, unborn, unknown,
  Student of our sweet English tongue,
Read out my words at night, alone:
  I was a poet, I was young.

Since I can never see your face,
  And never shake you by the hand,
I send my soul through time and space
  To greet you. You will understand.

RIOUPEROUX

High and solemn mountains guard Riouperoux,
- Small untidy village where the river drives a mill:
Frail as wood anemones, white and frail were you,
And drooping a little, like the slender daffodil.

Oh I will go to France again, and tramp the valley through,
And I will change these gentle clothes for clog and corduroy,
And work with the mill-hands of black Riouperoux,
And walk with you, and talk with you, like any other boy.

THE TOWN WITHOUT A MARKET

There lies afar behind a western hill
The Town without a Market, white and still;
For six feet long and not a third as high
Are those small habitations. There stood I,
Waiting to hear the citizens beneath
Murmur and sigh and speak through tongueless teeth.
When all the world lay burning in the sun
I heard their voices speak to me. Said one:
"Bright lights I loved and colours, I who find
That death is darkness, and has struck me blind."
Another cried: "I used to sing and play,
But here the world is silent, day by day."
And one: "On earth I could not see or hear,
But with my fingers touched what I was near,
And knew things round and soft, and brass from gold,
And dipped my hand in water, to feel cold,
And thought the grave would cure me, and was glad
When the time came to lose what joy I had."
Soon all the voices of a hundred dead
Shouted in wrath together. Someone said,
"I care not, but the girl was sweet to kiss
At evening in the meadows." "Hard it is"
Another cried, "to hear no hunting horn.
Ah me! the horse, the hounds, and the great grey morn
When I rode out a-hunting." And one sighed,
"I did not see my son before I died."
A boy said, "I was strong and swift to run:
Now they have tied my feet: what have I done?"
A man, "But it was good to arm and fight
And storm their cities in the dead of night."
An old man said, "I read my books all day,
But death has taken all my books away."
And one, "The popes and prophets did not well
To cheat poor dead men with false hopes of hell.
Better the whips of fire that hiss and rend
Than painless void proceeding to no end."
I smiled to hear them restless, I who sought
Peace. For I had not loved, I had not fought,

And books are vanities, and manly strength
A gathered flower. God grant us peace at length!
I heard no more, and turned to leave their town
Before the chill came, and the sun went down.
Then rose a whisper, and I seemed to know
A timorous man, buried long years ago.
"On Earth I used to shape the Thing that seems.
Master of all men, give me back my dreams.
Give me that world that never failed me then,
The hills I made and peopled with tall men,
The palace that I built and called my home,
My cities which could break the pride of Rome,
The three queens hidden in the sacred tree,
And those white cloudy folk who sang to me.
O death, why hast thou covered me so deep?
I was thy sister's child, the friend of Sleep."

Then said my heart, Death takes and cannot give.
Dark with no dream is hateful: let me live!

THE BALLAD OF CAMDEN TOWN

I walked with Maisie long years back
  The streets of Camden Town,
I splendid in my suit of black,
  And she divine in brown.

Hers was a proud and noble face,
  A secret heart, and eyes
Like water in a lonely place
  Beneath unclouded skies.

A bed, a chest, a faded mat,
  And broken chairs a few,
Were all we had to grace our flat
  In Hazel Avenue.

But I could walk to Hampstead Heath,
  And crown her head with daisies,
And watch the streaming world beneath,
  And men with other Maisies.

When I was ill and she was pale
  And empty stood our store,
She left the latchkey on its nail,
  And saw me nevermore.

Perhaps she cast herself away
  Lest both of us should drown:
Perhaps she feared to die, as they
  Who die in Camden Town.

What came of her? The bitter nights
  Destroy the rose and lily,
And souls are lost among the lights
  Of painted Piccadilly.

What came of her? The river flows
  So deep and wide and stilly,
And waits to catch the fallen rose

And clasp the broken lily.

I dream she dwells in London still
   And breathes the evening air,
And often walk to Primrose Hill,
   And hope to meet her there.

Once more together we will live,
   For I will find her yet:
I have so little to forgive;
   So much, I can't forget.

MIGNON

Knowest thou the land where bloom the lemon trees,
And darkly gleam the golden oranges?
A gentle wind blows down from that blue sky;
Calm stands the myrtle and the laurel high.
Knowest thou the land? So far and fair!
Thou, whom I love, and I will wander there.

Knowest thou the house with all its rooms aglow,
And shining hall and columned portico?
The marble statues stand and look at me.
Alas, poor child, what have they done to thee?
Knowest thou the land? So far and fair.
My Guardian, thou and I will wander there.

Knowest thou the mountain with its bridge of cloud?
The mule plods warily: the white mists crowd.
Coiled in their caves the brood of dragons sleep;
The torrent hurls the rock from steep to steep.
Knowest thou the land? So far and fair.
Father, away! Our road is over there!

FELO DE SE

The song of a man who was dead
Ere any had heard of his song,
Or had seen this his ultimate song,
With the lines of it written in red,
And the sound of it steady and strong.
When you hear it, you know I am dead.

Not because I was weary of life
As pallid poets are:
My star was a conquering star,
My element strife.
I am young, I am strong, I am brave,
It is therefore I go to the grave.

Now to life and to life's desire,
And to youth and the glory of youth,
Farewell, for I go to acquire,
By the one road left me, Truth.
Though a great God slay me with fire
I will shout till he answer me. Why?
(One soul and a Universe, why?)
And for this it is pleasant to die.

For years and years I have slumbered,
And slumber was heavy and sweet,
But the last few moments are numbered
Like trampling feet that beat.
I shall walk with the stars in their courses,
And hear very soon, very soon,
The voice of the forge of the Forces,
And ride on a ridge of the moon,
And sing a celestial tune.

TENEBRIS INTERLUCENTEM

A linnet who had lost her way
Sang on a blackened bough in Hell,
Till all the ghosts remembered well
The trees, the wind, the golden day.

At last they knew that they had died
When they heard music in that land,
And someone there stole forth a hand
To draw a brother to his side.

INVITATION
TO A YOUNG BUT LEARNED FRIEND TO ABANDON
ARCHAEOLOGY FOR THE MOMENT, AND
PLAY ONCE MORE WITH HIS NEGLECTED MUSE.

In those good days when we were young and wise,
You spake to music, you with the thoughtful eyes,
And God looked down from heaven, pleased to hear
A young man's song arise so firm and clear.
Has Fancy died? The Morning Star gone cold?
Why are you silent? Have we grown so old?
Must I alone keep playing? Will not you,
Lord of the Measures, string your lyre anew?
Lover of Greece, is this the richest store
You bring us,—withered leaves and dusty lore,
And broken vases widowed of their wine,
To brand you pedant while you stand divine?
Decorous words beseem the learned lip,
But Poets have the nicer scholarship.

In English glades they watch the Cyprian glow,
And all the Maenad melodies they know.
They hear strange voices in a London street,
And track the silver gleam of rushing feet;
And these are things that come not to the view
Of slippered dons who read a codex through.
   O honeyed Poet, will you praise no more
The moonlit garden and the midnight shore?
Brother, have you forgotten how to sing
The story of that weak and cautious king
Who reigned two hundred years in Trebizond?
You who would ever strive to pierce beyond
Love's ecstacy, Life's vision, is it well
We should not know the tales you have to tell?

BALLAD OF THE LONDONER

Evening falls on the smoky walls,
  And the railings drip with rain,
And I will cross the old river
  To see my girl again.

The great and solemn-gliding tram,
  Love's still-mysterious car,
Has many a light of gold and white,
  And a single dark red star.

I know a garden in a street
  Which no one ever knew;
I know a rose beyond the Thames,
  Where flowers are pale and few.

THE FIRST SONNET OF BATHROLAIRE

Over the moonless land of Bathrolaire
Rises at night, when revelry begins,
A white unreal orb, a sun that spins,
A sun that watches with a sullen stare
That dance spasmodic they are dancing there,
Whilst drone and cry and drone of violins
Hint at the sweetness of forgotten sins,
Or call the devotees of shame to prayer.
And all the spaces of the midnight town
Ring with appeal and sorrowful abuse.
There some most lonely are: some try to crown
Mad lovers with sad boughs of formal yews,
And Titan women wandering up and down
Lead on the pale fanatics of the muse.

THE SECOND SONNET OF BATHROLAIRE

Now the sweet Dawn on brighter fields afar
Has walked among the daisies, and has breathed
The glory of the mountain winds, and sheathed
The stubborn sword of Night's last-shining star.
In Bathrolaire when Day's old doors unbar
The motley mask, fantastically wreathed,
Pass through a strong portcullis brazen teethed,
And enter glowing mines of cinnabar.
Stupendous prisons shut them out from day,
Gratings and caves and rayless catacombs,
And the unrelenting rack and tourniquet
Grind death in cells where jetting gaslight gloams,
And iron ladders stretching far away
Dive to the depths of those eternal domes.

THE MASQUE OF THE MAGI

Three Kings have come to Bethlehem
With a trailing star in front of them.

MARY

What would you in this little place,
   You three bright kings?

KINGS

Mother, we tracked the trailing star
Which brought us here from lands afar,
And we would look on his dear face
Round whom the Seraphs fold their wings.

MARY

But who are you, bright kings?

CASPAR

Caspar am I: the rocky North
From storm and silence drave me forth
   Down to the blue and tideless sea.
I do not fear the tinkling sword,
For I am a great battle-lord,
   And love the horns of chivalry.
And I have brought thee splendid gold,
The strong man's joy, refined and cold.
   All hail, thou Prince of Galilee!

BALTHAZAR

I am Balthazar, Lord of Ind,
Where blows a soft and scented wind
   From Taprobane towards Cathay.
My children, who are tall and wise,
Stand by a tree with shutten eyes

And seem to meditate or pray.
And these red drops of frankincense
Betoken man's intelligence.
   Hail, Lord of Wisdom, Prince of Day!

MELCHIOR

I am the dark man, Melchior,
And I shall live but little more
   Since I am old and feebly move.
My kingdom is a burnt-up land
Half buried by the drifting sand,
   So hot Apollo shines above.
What could I bring but simple myrrh
White blossom of the cordial fire?
   Hail, Prince of Souls, and Lord of Love!

CHORUS OF ANGELS

O Prince of souls and Lord of Love,
O'er thee the purple-breasted dove
Shall watch with open silver wings,
   Thou King of Kings.
Suaviole o flos Virginum,
Apparuit Rex Gentium.
. . .
"Who art thou, little King of Kings?"
His wondering mother sings.

THE BALLAD OF HAMPSTEAD HEATH

From Heaven's Gate to Hampstead Heath
  Young Bacchus and his crew
Came tumbling down, and o'er the town
  Their bursting trumpets blew.

The silver night was wildly bright,
  And madly shone the Moon
To hear a song so clear and strong,
  With such a lovely tune.

From London's houses, huts and flats,
  Came busmen, snobs, and Earls,
And ugly men in bowler hats
  With charming little girls.

Sir Moses came with eyes of flame,
  Judd, who is like a bloater,
The brave Lord Mayor in coach and pair,
  King Edward, in his motor.

Far in a rosy mist withdrawn
  The God and all his crew,
Silenus pulled by nymphs, a faun,
  A satyr drenched in dew,

Smiled as they wept those shining tears
  Only Immortals know,
Whose feet are set among the stars,
  Above the shifting snow.

And one spake out into the night,
  Before they left for ever,
"Rejoice, rejoice!" and his great voice
  Rolled like a splendid river.

He spake in Greek, which Britons speak
  Seldom, and circumspectly;
But Mr. Judd, that man of mud,

16

Translated it correctly.

And when they heard that happy word,
  Policemen leapt and ambled:
The busmen pranced, the maidens danced,
  The men in bowlers gambolled.

A wistful Echo stayed behind
  To join the mortal dances,
But Mr Judd, with words unkind,
  Rejected her advances.

And passing down through London Town
  She stopped, for all was lonely,
Attracted by a big brass plate
  Inscribed, FOR MEMBERS ONLY.

And so she went to Parliament,
  But those ungainly men
Woke up from sleep, and turned about,
  And fell asleep again.

LITANY TO SATAN (from Baudelaire.)

O grandest of the Angels, and most wise,
O fallen God, fate-driven from the skies,
Satan, at last take pity on our pain.

O first of exiles who endurest wrong,
Yet growest, in thy hatred, still more strong,
Satan, at last take pity on our pain!

O subterranean King, omniscient,
Healer of man's immortal discontent,
Satan, at last take pity on our pain.

To lepers and to outcasts thou dost show
That Passion is the Paradise below.
Satan, at last take pity on our pain.

Thou by thy mistress Death hast given to man
Hope, the imperishable courtesan.
Satan, at last take pity on our pain.

Thou givest to the Guilty their calm mien
Which damns the crowd around the guillotine.
Satan, at last take pity on our pain.

Thou knowest the corners of the jealous Earth
Where God has hidden jewels of great worth.
Satan, at last take pity on our pain.

Thou dost discover by mysterious signs
Where sleep the buried people of the mines.
Satan, at last take pity on our pain.

Thou stretchest forth a saving hand to keep
Such men as roam upon the roofs in sleep.
Satan, at last take pity on our pain.

Thy power can make the halting Drunkard's feet
Avoid the peril of the surging street.

Satan, at last take pity on our pain.

Thou, to console our helplessness, didst plot
The cunning use of powder and of shot.
Satan, at last take pity on our pain.

Thy awful name is written as with pitch
On the unrelenting foreheads of the rich.
Satan, at last take pity on our pain.

In strange and hidden places thou dost move
Where women cry for torture in their love.
Satan, at last take pity on our pain.

Father of those whom God's tempestuous ire
Has flung from Paradise with sword and fire,
Satan, at last take pity on our pain.

PRAYER

Satan, to thee be praise upon the Height
Where thou wast king of old, and in the night
Of Hell, where thou dost dream on silently.
Grant that one day beneath the Knowledge-tree,
When it shoots forth to grace thy royal brow,
My soul may sit, that cries upon thee now.

THE TRANSLATOR AND THE CHILDREN

While I translated Baudelaire,
Children were playing out in the air.
Turning to watch, I saw the light
That made their clothes and faces bright.
I heard the tune they meant to sing
As they kept dancing in a ring;
But I could not forget my book,
And thought of men whose faces shook
When babies passed them with a look.

They are as terrible as death,
Those children in the road beneath.
Their witless chatter is more dread
Than voices in a madman's head:
Their dance more awful and inspired,
Because their feet are never tired,
Than silent revel with soft sound
Of pipes, on consecrated ground,
When all the ghosts go round and round.

OPPORTUNITY (from Machiavelli.)

"But who art thou, with curious beauty graced,
O woman, stamped with some bright heavenly seal
Why go thy feet on wings, and in such haste?"

"I am that maid whose secret few may steal,
Called Opportunity. I hasten by
Because my feet are treading on a wheel,

Being more swift to run than birds to fly.
And rightly on my feet my wings I wear,
To blind the sight of those who track and spy;

Rightly in front I hold my scattered hair
To veil my face, and down my breast to fall,
Lest men should know my name when I am there;

And leave behind my back no wisp at all
For eager folk to clutch, what time I glide
So near, and turn, and pass beyond recall."

"Tell me; who is that Figure at thy side?"
"Penitence. Mark this well that by decree
Who lets me go must keep her for his bride.

And thou hast spent much time in talk with me
Busied with thoughts and fancies vainly grand,
Nor hast remarked, O fool, neither dost see
How lightly I have fled beneath thy hand."

DESTROYER OF SHIPS, MEN, CITIES

Helen of Troy has sprung from Hell
  To claim her ancient throne,
So we have bidden friends farewell
  To follow her alone.

The Lady of the laurelled brow,
  The Queen of pride and power,
Looks rather like a phantom now,
  And rather like a flower.

Deep in her eyes the lamp of night
  Burns with a secret flame,
Where shadows pass that have no sight,
  And ghosts that have no name.

For mute is battle's brazen horn
  That rang for Priest and King,
And she who drank of that brave morn
  Is pale with evening.

An hour there is when bright words flow,
  A little hour for sleep,
An hour between, when lights are low,
  And then she seems to weep,

But no less lovely than of old
  She shines, and almost hears
The horns that blew in days of gold,
  The shouting charioteers.

And still she breaks the hearts of men,
  Their hearts and all their pride,
Doomed to be cruel once again,
  And live dissatisfied.

WAR SONG OF THE SARACENS

We are they who come faster than fate: we are they who ride early
    or late:
We storm at your ivory gate: Pale Kings of the Sunset, beware!
Not on silk nor in samet we lie, not in curtained solemnity die
Among women who chatter and cry, and children who mumble a
    prayer.
But we sleep by the ropes of the camp, and we rise with a shout, and
    we tramp
With the sun or the moon for a lamp, and the spray of the wind in
    our hair.

From the lands, where the elephants are, to the forts of Merou and
Balghar,
Our steel we have brought and our star to shine on the ruins of Rum.
We have marched from the Indus to Spain, and by God we will go
    there again;
We have stood on the shore of the plain where the Waters of Destiny
    boom.

A mart of destruction we made at Jalula where men were afraid,
For death was a difficult trade, and the sword was a broker of doom;
And the Spear was a Desert Physician who cured not a few of
    ambition,
And drave not a few to perdition with medicine bitter and strong:
And the shield was a grief to the fool and as bright as a desolate
    pool,
And as straight as the rock of Stamboul when their cavalry
    thundered along:
For the coward was drowned with the brave when our battle
sheered up like a wave,
And the dead to the desert we gave, and the glory to God in our
    song.

JOSEPH AND MARY

JOSEPH

Mary, art thou the little maid
  Who plucked me flowers in Spring?
I know thee not: I feel afraid:
  Thou'rt strange this evening.

A sweet and rustic girl I won
  What time the woods were green;
No woman with deep eyes that shone,
  And the pale brows of a Queen.

MARY (inattentive to his words.)

A stranger came with feet of flame
  And told me this strange thing, -
For all I was a village maid
  My son should be a King.

JOSEPH

A King, dear wife. Who ever knew
  Of Kings in stables born!

MARY

Do you hear, in the dark and starlit blue
  The clarion and the horn?

JOSEPH

Mary, alas, lest grief and joy
  Have sent thy wits astray;
But let me look on this my boy,
  And take the wraps away.

MARY

Behold the lad.

JOSEPH

  I dare not gaze:
Light streams from every limb.

MARY

The winter sun has stored his rays,
  And passed the fire to him.

Look Eastward, look! I hear a sound.
  O Joseph, what do you see?

JOSEPH

The snow lies quiet on the ground
  And glistens on the tree;

The sky is bright with a star's great light,
  And clearly I behold
Three Kings descending yonder hill,
  Whose crowns are crowns of gold.

O Mary, what do you hear and see
  With your brow toward the West?

MARY

The snow lies glistening on the tree
  And silent on Earth's breast;

And strong and tall, with lifted eyes
  Seven shepherds walk this way,
And angels breaking from the skies
  Dance, and sing hymns, and pray.

JOSEPH

I wonder much at these bright Kings;
  The shepherds I despise.

MARY

You know not what a shepherd sings,
  Nor see his shining eyes.

NO COWARD'S SONG

I am afraid to think about my death,
When it shall be, and whether in great pain
I shall rise up and fight the air for breath
Or calmly wait the bursting of my brain.

I am no coward who could seek in fear
A folklore solace or sweet Indian tales:
I know dead men are deaf and cannot hear
The singing of a thousand nightingales.

I know dead men are blind and cannot see
The friend that shuts in horror their big eyes,
And they are witless—O I'd rather be
A living mouse than dead as a man dies.

A WESTERN VOYAGE

My friend the Sun—like all my friends
  Inconstant, lovely, far away -
Is out, and bright, and condescends
  To glory in our holiday.

A furious march with him I'll go
  And race him in the Western train,
And wake the hills of long ago
  And swim the Devon sea again.

I have done foolishly to head
  The footway of the false moonbeams,
To light my lamp and call the dead
  And read their long black printed dreams.

I have done foolishly to dwell
  With Fear upon her desert isle,
To take my shadowgraph to Hell,
  And then to hope the shades would smile.

And since the light must fail me soon
  (But faster, faster, Western train!)
Proud meadows of the afternoon,
  I have remembered you again.

And I'll go seek through moor and dale
  A flower that wastrel winds caress;
The bud is red and the leaves pale,
  The name of it Forgetfulness.

Then like the old and happy hills
  With frozen veins and fires outrun,
I'll wait the day when darkness kills
  My brother and good friend, the Sun.

FOUNTAINS

Soft is the collied night, and cool
The wind about the garden pool.
Here will I dip my burning hand
And move an inch of drowsy sand,
And pray the dark reflected skies
To fasten with their seal mine eyes.
A million million leagues away
Among the stars the goldfish play,
And high above the shadowed stars
Wave and float the nenuphars.

THE WELSH SEA

Far out across Carnarvon bay,
  Beneath the evening waves,
The ancient dead begin their day
  And stream among the graves.

Listen, for they of ghostly speech,
  Who died when Christ was born,
May dance upon the golden beach
  That once was golden corn.

And you may learn of Dyfed's reign,
  And dream Nemedian tales
Of Kings who sailed in ships from Spain
  And lent their swords to Wales.

Listen, for like a golden snake
  The Ocean twists and stirs,
And whispers how the dead men wake
  And call across the years.

OXFORD CANAL

When you have wearied of the valiant spires of this County Town,
Of its wide white streets and glistening museums, and black
  monastic walls,
Of its red motors and lumbering trains, and self-sufficient people,
I will take you walking with me to a place you have not seen -
Half town and half country—the land of the Canal.
It is dearer to me than the antique town: I love it more than the
  rounded hills:
Straightest, sublimest of rivers is the long Canal.
I have observed great storms and trembled: I have wept for fear of
  the dark.
But nothing makes me so afraid as the clear water of this idle canal
  on a summer s noon.
Do you see the great telegraph poles down in the water, how every
  wire is distinct?
If a body fell into the canal it would rest entangled in those wires for
  ever, between earth and air.
For the water is as deep as the stars are high.
One day I was thinking how if a man fell from that lofty pole
He would rush through the water toward me till his image was
  scattered by his splash,
When suddenly a train rushed by: the brazen dome of the engine
  flashed:
the long white carriages roared;
The sun veiled himself for a moment, and the signals loomed in fog;
A savage woman screamed at me from a barge: little children began
  to cry;
The untidy landscape rose to life: a sawmill started;
A cart rattled down to the wharf, and workmen clanged over the
  iron footbridge;
A beautiful old man nodded from the first story window of a square
  red house,
And a pretty girl came out to hang up clothes in a small delightful
  garden.
O strange motion in the suburb of a county town: slow regular
movement of the dance of death!
Men and not phantoms are these that move in light.
  Forgotten they live, and forgotten die.

HIALMAR SPEAKS TO THE RAVEN
from Leconte de Lisle

Night on the bloodstained snow: the wind is chill:
And there a thousand tombless warriors lie,
Grasping their swords, wild-featured. All are still.
Above them the black ravens wheel and cry.

A brilliant moon sends her cold light abroad:
Hialmar arises from the reddened slain,
Heavily leaning on his broken sword,
And bleeding from his side the battle-rain.

"Hail to you all: is there one breath still drawn
Among those fierce and fearless lads who played
So merrily, and sang as sweet in the dawn
As thrushes singing in the bramble shade?

"They have no word to say: my helm's unbound,
My breastplate by the axe unriveted:
Blood's on my eyes; I hear a spreading sound,
Like waves or wolves that clamour in my head.

"Eater of men, old raven, come this way,
And with thine iron bill open my breast:
To-morrow find us where we lie to-day,
And bear my heart to her that I love best.

"Through Upsala, where drink the Jarls and sing,
And clash their golden bowls in company,
Bird of the moor, carry on tireless wing
To Ylmer's daughter there the heart of me.

"And thou shalt see her standing straight and pale,
High pedestalled on some rook-haunted tower:
She has two earrings, silver and vermeil,
And eyes like stars that shine in sunset hour.

"Tell her my love, thou dark bird ominous;
Give her my heart, no bloodless heart and vile

But red compact and strong, O raven. Thus
Shall Ylmer's daughter greet thee with a smile.

"Now let my life from twenty deep wounds flow,
And wolves may drink the blood. My time is done.
Young, brave and spotless, I rejoice to go
And sit where all the Gods are, in the sun."

THE BALLAD OF THE STUDENT IN THE SOUTH

It was no sooner than this morn
  That first I found you there,
Deep in a field of southern corn
  As golden as your hair.

I had read books you had not read,
  Yet I was put to shame
To hear the simple words you said,
  And see your eyes aflame.

Shall I forget when prying dawn
  Sends me about my way,
The careless stars, the quiet lawn,
  And you with whom I lay?

Your's is the beauty of the moon,
  The wisdom of the sea,
Since first you tasted, sweet and soon,
  Of God's forbidden tree.

Darling, a scholar's fancies sink
  So faint beneath your song;
And you are right, why should we think,
  We who are young and strong?

For we are simple, you and I,
  We do what others do,
Linger and toil and laugh and die
  And love the whole night through.

THE QUEEN'S SONG

Had I the power
  To Midas given of old
To touch a flower
  And leave the petals gold
I then might touch thy face,
  Delightful boy,
And leave a metal grace,
  A graven joy.

Thus would I slay, -
  Ah, desperate device!
The vital day
  That trembles in thine eyes,
And let the red lips close
  Which sang so well,
And drive away the rose
  To leave a shell.

Then I myself,
  Rising austere and dumb
On the hight shelf
  Of my half-lighted room,
Would place the shining bust
  And wait alone,
Until I was but dust,
  Buried unknown.

Thus in my love
  For nations yet unborn,
I would remove
  From our two lives the morn,
And muse on loveliness
  In mine armchair,
Content should Time confess
  How sweet you were.

LORD ARNALDOS
Quien hubiese tal ventura?

The strangest of adventures,
That happen by the sea,
Befell to Lord Arnaldos
On the Evening of St. John;
For he was out a hunting -
A huntsman bold was he! -
When he beheld a little ship
And close to land was she.
Her cords were all of silver,
Her sails of cramasy;
And he who sailed the little ship
Was singing at the helm;
The waves stood still to hear him,
The wind was soft and low;
The fish who dwell in darkness
Ascended through the sea,
And all the birds in heaven
Flew down to his mast-tree.
Then spake the Lord Arnaldos,
(Well shall you hear his words!)
"Tell me for God's sake, sailor,
What song may that song be?"
The sailor spake in answer,
And answer thus made he; -
"I only tell my song to those
Who sail away with me."

WE THAT WERE FRIENDS

We that were friends to-night have found
A sudden fear, a secret flame:
I am on fire with that soft sound
You make, in uttering my name.

Forgive a young and boastful man
Whom dreams delight and passions please,
And love me as great women can
Who have no children at their knees.

MY FRIEND

I had a friend who battled for the truth
With stubborn heart and obstinate despair,
Till all his beauty left him, and his youth,
And there were few to love him anywhere.

Then would he wander out among the graves,
And think of dead men lying in a row;
Or, standing on a cliff observe the waves,
And hear the wistful sound of winds below;

And yet they told him nothing. So he sought
The twittering forest at the break of day,
Or on fantastic mountains shaped a thought
As lofty and impenitent as they.

And next he went in wonder through a town
Slowly by day and hurriedly by night,
And watched men walking up the street and down
With timorous and terrible delight.

Weary, he drew man's wisdom from a book,
And pondered on the high words spoken of old,
Pacing a lamplit room: but soon forsook
The golden sentences that left him cold.

After, a woman found him, and his head
Lay on her breast, till he forgot his pain
In gentle kisses on a midnight bed,
And welcomed royal-winged joy again.

When love became a loathing, as it must,
He knew not where to turn; and he was wise,
Being now old, to sink among the dust,
And rest his rebel heart, and close his eyes.

IDEAL

When all my gentle friends had gone
I wandered in the night alone:
Beneath the green electric glare
I saw men pass with hearts of stone.
Yet still I heard them everywhere,
Those golden voices of the air:
"Friend, we will go to hell with thee,
Thy griefs, thy glories we will share,
And rule the earth, and bind the sea,
And set ten thousand devils free;—"
"What dost thou, stranger, at my side,
Thou gaunt old man accosting me?
Away, this is my night of pride!
On lunar seas my boat will glide
And I shall know the secret things."
The old man answered: "Woe betide!"
Said I "The world was made for kings:
To him who works and working sings
Come joy and majesty and power
And steadfast love with royal wings."
"O watch these fools that blink and cower,"
Said that wise man: "and every hour
A score is born, a dozen dies."
Said I: —"In London fades the flower;
But far away the bright blue skies
Shall watch my solemn walls arise,
And all the glory, all the grace
Of earth shall gather there, and eyes
Will shine like stars in that new place."
Said he. "Indeed of ancient race
Thou comest, with thy hollow scheme.
But sail, O architect of dream,
To lands beyond the Ocean stream.
Where are the islands of the blest,
And where Atlantis, where Theleme?"

MARY MAGDALEN

O eyes that strip the souls of men!
There came to me the Magdalen.
Her blue robe with a cord was bound,
Her hair with Lenten lilies crowned.
"Arise," she said "God calls for thee,
Turned to new paths thy feet must be.
Leave the fever and the feast
Leave the friend thou lovest best:
For thou must walk in barefoot ways,
To give my dear Lord Jesus praise."

Then answered I—"Sweet Magdalen,
God's servant, once beloved of men,
Why didst thou change old ways for new,
Thy trailing red for corded blue,
Roses for lilies on thy brow,
Rich splendour for a barren vow?"

Gentle of speech she answered me:-
"Sir, I was sick with revelry.
True, I have scarred the night with sin,
A pale and tawdry heroine;
But once I heard a voice that said
'Who lives in sin is surely dead,
But whoso turns to follow me
Hath joy and immortality.'"

"O Mary, not for this," I cried,
"Didst thou renounce thy scented pride.
Not for a taste of endless years
Or barren joy apart from tears
Didst thou desert the courts of men.
Tell me thy truth, sweet Magdalen!"

She trembled, and her eyes grew dim:-
"For love of Him, for love of Him."

I ROSE FROM DREAMLESS HOURS

I rose from dreamless hours and sought the morn
That beat upon my window: from the sill
I watched sweet lands, where Autumn light newborn
Swayed through the trees and lingered on the hill.
If things so lovely are, why labour still
To dream of something more than this I see?
Do I remember tales of Galilee,
I who have slain my faith and freed my will?
Let me forget dead faith, dead mystery,
Dead thoughts of things I cannot comprehend.
Enough the light mysterious in the tree,
Enough the friendship of my chosen friend.

PRAYER

Let me not know how sins and sorrows glide
Along the sombre city of our rage,
Or why the sons of men are heavy-eyed.

Let me not know, except from printed page,
The pain of litter love, of baffled pride,
Or sickness shadowing with a long presage.

Let me not know, since happy some have died
Quickly in youth or quietly in age,
How faint, how loud the bravest hearts have cried.

A MIRACLE OF BETHLEHEM

SCENE: A street of that village.
Three men with ropes, accosted by a stranger.

THE STRANGER

I pray you, tell me where you go
With heads averted from the skies,
And long ropes trailing in the snow,
And resolution in your eyes.

THE FIRST MAN

I am a lover sick of love,
For scorn rewards my constancy;
And now I hate the stars above,
Because my dear will naught of me.

THE SECOND MAN

I am a beggar man, and play
Songs with a splendid swing in them,
But I have seen no food to-day.
They want no song in Bethlehem.

THE THIRD MAN

I am an old man, Sir, and blind,
A child of darkness since my birth.
I cannot even call to mind
The beauty of the scheme of earth.

Therefore I sought to understand
A secret hid from mortal eyes,
So in a far and fragrant land
I talked with men accounted wise,

And I implored the Indian priest
For wisdom from his holy snake,

Yet am no wiser in the least,
And have not seen the darkness break.

STRANGER

And whither go ye now, unhappy three?

THE THREE MEN WITH ROPES

Sir, in our strange and special misery
We met this night, and swore in bitter pride
To sing one song together, friend with friend,
And then, proceeding to the country side,
To bind this cordage to a barren tree,
And face to face to give our lives an end,
And only thus shall we be satisfied.
  (They make to continue their road)

THE STRANGER

Stay for a moment. Great is your despair,
But God is kind. What voice from over there?

A WOMAN (from a lattice)

My lover, O my lover, come to me!

FIRST MAN

God with you. (he runs to the window)

STRANGER

Ah, how swiftly gone is he!

MANY VOICES, (heard singing in a cottage)

There is a softness in the night
A wonder in that splendid star
That fills us with delight,
Poor foolish working people that we are,
And only fit to keep
A little garden or a dozen sheep.

Old broken women at the fire
Have many ancient tales they sing,
How the whole world's desire
Should blossom here, and how a child should bring
New glory to his race
Though born in so contemptible a place.

Let all come in, if any brother go
In shame or hunger, cold or fear,
Through all this waste of snow.
To night the Star, the Rose, the Song are near,
And still inside the door
Is full provision for another score.
(The Beggar runs to them)

THE STRANGER (to the Blind Man)

Do you not mean to share these joys?

THE BLIND MAN

Aweary of this earthly noise
I pace my silent way.
Come you and help me tie this rope:
I would not lose my only hope.
Already clear the birds I hear,
Already breaks the day.

STRANGER

O foolish and most blind old man,
Where are those other two?

THE BLIND MAN

Why, one is wed and t'other fed:
Small thanks they gave to you.

STRANGER

To me no thanks are due.
Yet since I have some little power
Bequeathed me at this holy hour,

I tell you, friend, that God shall grant
This night to you your dearest want.

THE BLIND MAN

Why this sweet odour? Why this flame?
I am afraid. What is your name?

THE STRANGER

Ask your desire, for this great night
Is passing.

THE BLIND MAN

Sir, I ask my sight.

THE STRANGER

To see this earth? Or would you see
That hidden world which sent you me?

THE BLIND MAN

O sweet it were but once before I die
To track the bird about the windy sky,
Or watch the soft and changing grace
Imprinted on a human face.
Yet grant me that which most I struggled for,
Since I am old, and snow is on the ground.
On earth there's little to be found,
And I would bear with earth no more.
O gentle youth,
A fool am I, but let me see the Truth!

THE STRANGER

Gaze in my eyes.

THE BLIND MAN

   How can I gaze?
What song is that, and what these rays

Of splendour and this rush of wings?

THE STRANGER

These are the new celestial things.

THE BLIND MAN

Round the body of a child
A great dark flame runs wild.
What may this be?

THE STRANGER

Look further, you shall see.

THE BLIND MAN

Out on the sea of time and far away
The Empires sail like ships, and many years
Scatter before them in a mist of spray:
Beyond is mist—when the mist clears -
Enough—Away!—O friend, I would be there!

STRANGER

It is most sure that God has heard his prayer.
(The stranger vanishes)

THE BEGGAR

(Leading a troop of revellers from the house where they were
singing)

Come, brothers, seek my friend and bring him in.
On such a night as this it were a sin
To leave the blind alone.

THE REVELLERS

Greatly we fear lest he, still resolute,
Have wandered to the fields for poisoned fruit.

THE BEGGAR

See here upon this stone . . .
He is all frozen . . . take him to a bed
And warm his hands.

THE REVELLERS

O sorrow, he is dead!

GRAVIS DULCIS IMMUTABILIS

Come, let me kiss your wistful face
Where Sorrow curves her bow of pain,
And live sweet days and bitter days
With you, or wanting you again.

I dread your perishable gold:
Come near me now; the years are few.
Alas, when you and I are old
I shall not want to look at you:

And yet come in. I shall not dare
To gaze upon your countenance,
But I shall huddle in my chair,
Turn to the fire my fireless glance,

And listen, while that slow and grave
Immutable sweet voice of yours
Rises and falls, as falls a wave
In summer on forgotten shores.

PILLAGE

They will trample our gardens to mire, they will bury our city in fire;
Our women await their desire, our children the clang of the chain.
Our grave-eyed judges and lords they will bind by the neck with
cords,
And harry with whips and swords till they perish of shame or pain,
And the great lapis lazuli dome where the gods of our race had a
home
Will break like a wave from the foam, and shred into fiery rain.

No more on the long summer days shall we walk in the meadow-
sweet ways
With the teachers of music and phrase, and the masters of dance and
design.
No more when the trumpeter calls shall we feast in the white-light
halls;
For stayed are the soft footfalls of the moon-browed bearers of wine,
And lost are the statues of Kings and of Gods with great glorious
wings,
And an empire of beautiful things, and the lips of the love who was
mine.

We have vanished, but not into night, though our manhood we sold
to
delight,
Neglecting the chances of fight, unfit for the spear and the bow.
We are dead, but our living was great: we are dumb, but a song of
our
State
Will roam in the desert and wait, with its burden of long, long ago,
Till a scholar from sea-bright lands unearth from the years and the
sands
Some image with beautiful hands, and know what we want him to
know.

THE BALLAD OF ZACHO
(a Greek Legend.)

Zacho the King rode out of old
  (And truth is what I tell)
With saddle and spurs and a rein of gold
  To find the door of Hell.

And round around him surged the dead
  With soft and lustrous eyes.
"Why came you here, old friend?" they said:
  "Unwise . . . unwise . . . unwise!

"You should have left to the prince your son
  Spurs and saddle and rein:
Your bright and morning days are done;
  You ride not out again."

"I came to greet my friends who fell
  Sword-scattered from my side;
And when I've drunk the wine of Hell
  I'll out again and ride!"

But Charon rose and caught his hair
  In fingers sharp and long.
"Loose me, old ferryman: play fair:
  Try if my arm be strong."

Thrice drave he hard on Charon's breast,
  And struck him thrice to ground,
Till stranger ghosts came out o' the west
  And sat like stars around.

And thrice old Charon rose up high
  And seized him as before.
"Loose me! a broken man am I,
  And fight with you no more."

"Zacho, arise, my home is near;
  I pray you walk with me:

I've hung my tent so full of fear
   You well may shake to see.

"Home to my home come they who fight,
   Who fight but not to win:
Without, my tent is black as night,
   And red as fire within.

"Though winds blow cold and I grow old,
   My tent is fast and fair:
The pegs are dead men's stout right arms,
   The cords, their golden hair."

PAVLOVNA IN LONDON

I listened to the hunger-hearted clown,
  Sadder than he: I heard a woman sing, -
A tall dark woman in a scarlet gown -
  And saw those golden toys the jugglers fling.
I found a tawdry room and there sat I,
  There angled for each murmur soft and strange,
    The pavement-cries from darkness and below:
I watched the drinkers laugh, the lovers sigh,
  And thought how little all the world would change
    If clowns were audience, and we the Show.

What starry music are they playing now?
  What dancing in this dreary theatre?
Who is she with the moon upon her brow,
  And who the fire-foot god that follows her? -
Follows among those unbelieved-in trees
  Back-shadowing in their parody of light
    Across the little cardboard balustrade;
And we, like that poor Faun who pipes and flees,
  Adore their beauty, hate it for too bright,
    And tremble, half in rapture, half afraid.

Play on, O furtive and heartbroken Faun!
  What is your thin dull pipe for such as they?
I know you blinded by the least white dawn,
  And dare you face their quick and quivering Day?
Dare you, like us, weak but undaunted men,
  Reliant on some deathless spark in you
    Turn your dull eyes to what the gods desire,
Touch the light finger of your goddess; then
  After a second's flash of gold and blue,
    Drunken with that divinity, expire?

O dance, Diana, dance, Endymion,
  Till calm ancestral shadows lay their hands
Gently across mine eyes: in days long gone
  Have I not danced with gods in garden lands?
I too a wild unsighted atom borne

Deep in the heart of some heroic boy
  Span in the dance ten thousand years ago,
And while his young eyes glittered in the morn
  Something of me felt something of his joy,
    And longed to rule a body, and to know.

Singer long dead and sweeter-lipped than I,
  In whose proud line the soul-dark phrases burn,
Would you could praise their passionate symmetry,
  Who loved the colder shapes, the Attic urn.
But your far song, my faint one, what are they,
  And what their dance and faery thoughts and ours,
    Or night abloom with splendid stars and pale?
'Tis an old story that sweet flowers decay,
  And dreams, the noblest, die as soon as flowers,
    And dancers, all the world of them, must fail.

THE SENTIMENTALIST

There lies a photograph of you
    Deep in a box of broken things.
This was the face I loved and knew
    Five years ago, when life had wings;

Five years ago, when through a town
    Of bright and soft and shadowy bowers
We walked and talked and trailed our gown
    Regardless of the cinctured hours.

The precepts that we held I kept;
    Proudly my ways with you I went:
We lived our dreams while others slept,
    And did not shrink from sentiment.

Now I go East and you stay West
    And when between us Europe lies
I shall forget what I loved best
    Away from lips and hands and eyes.

But we were Gods then: we were they
    Who laughed at fools, believed in friends,
And drank to all that golden day
    Before us, which this poem ends.

DON JUAN IN HELL
(from Baudelaire.)

The night Don Juan came to pay his fees
  To Charon, by the caverned water's shore,
A beggar, proud-eyed as Antisthenes,
  Stretched out his knotted fingers on the oar.

Mournful, with drooping breasts and robes unsewn
  The shapes of women swayed in ebon skies,
Trailing behind him with a restless moan
  Like cattle herded for a sacrifice.

Here, grinning for his wage, stood Sganarelle,
  And here Don Luis pointed, bent and dim,
To show the dead who lined the holes of Hell,
  This was that impious son who mocked at him.

The hollow-eyed, the chaste Elvira came,
  Trembling and veiled, to view her traitor spouse.
Was it one last bright smile she thought to claim,
  Such as made sweet the morning of his vows?

A great stone man rose like a tower on board,
  Stood at the helm and cleft the flood profound:
But the calm hero, leaning on his sword,
  Gazed back, and would not offer one look round.

THE BALLAD OF ISKANDER

Aflatun and Aristu and King Iskander
Are Plato, Aristotle, Alexander.

Sultan Iskander sat him down
On his golden throne, in his golden crown,
And shouted, "Wine and flute-girls three,
And the Captain, ho! of my ships at sea."

He drank his bowl of wine; he kept
The flute-girls dancing till they wept,
Praised and kissed their painted lips,
And turned to the Captain of All his Ships

And cried, "O Lord of my Ships that go
From the Persian Gulf to the Pits of Snow,
Inquire for men unknown to man!"
Said Sultan Iskander of Yoonistan.

"Daroosh is dead, and I am King
Of Everywhere and Everything:
Yet leagues and leagues away for sure
The lion-hearted dream of war.

"Admiral, I command you sail!
Take you a ship of silver mail,
And fifty sailors, young and bold,
And stack provision deep in the hold,

"And seek out twenty men that know
All babel tongues which flaunt and flow;
And stay! Impress those learned two,
Old Aflatun, and Aristu.

"And set your prow South-western ways
A thousand bright and dimpling days,
And find me lion-hearted Lords
With breasts to feed Our rusting swords."

The Captain of the Ships bowed low.
"Sir," he replied, "I will do so."
And down he rode to the harbour mouth,
To choose a boat to carry him South.

And he launched a ship of silver mail,
With fifty lads to hoist the sail,
And twenty wise—all tongues they knew,
And Aflatun, and Aristu.

There had not dawned the second day
But the glittering galleon sailed away,
And through the night like one great bell
The marshalled armies sang farewell.

In twenty days the silver ship
Had passed the Isle of Serendip,
And made the flat Araunian coasts
Inhabited, at noon, by Ghosts.

In thirty days the ship was far
Beyond the land of Calcobar,
Where men drink Dead Men's Blood for wine,
And dye their beards alizarine.

But on the hundredth day there came
Storm with his windy wings aflame,
And drave them out to that Lone Sea
Whose shores are near Eternity.

* * *

For seven years and seven years
Sailed those forgotten mariners,
Nor could they spy on either hand
The faintest level of good red land.

Bird or fish they saw not one;
There swam no ship beside their own,
And day-night long the lilied Deep
Lay round them, with its flowers asleep.

The beams began to warp and crack,

The silver plates turned filthy black,
And drooping down on the carven rails
Hung those once lovely silken sails.

And all the great ship's crew who were
Such noble lads to do and dare
Grew old and tired of the changeless sky
And laid them down on the deck to die.

And they who spake all tongues there be
Made antics with solemnity,
Or closely huddled each to each
Talked ribald in a foreign speech.

And Aflatun and Aristu
Let their Beards grow, and their Beards grew
Round and about the mainmast tree
Where they stood still, and watched the sea.

And day by day their Captain grey
Knelt on the rotting poop to pray:
And yet despite ten thousand prayers
They saw no ship that was not theirs.

* * *

When thrice the seven years had passed
They saw a ship, a ship at last!
Untarnished glowed its silver mail,
Windless bellied its silken sail.

With a shout the grizzled sailors rose
Cursing the years of sick repose,
And they who spake in tongues unknown
Gladly reverted to their own.

The Captain leapt and left his prayers
And hastened down the dust-dark stairs,
And taking to hand a brazen Whip
He woke to life the long dead ship.

But Aflatun and Aristu,
Who had no work that they could do,

Gazed at the stranger Ship and Sea
With their beards around the mainmast tree.

Nearer and nearer the new boat came,
Till the hands cried out on the old ship's shame -
"Silken sail to a silver boat,
We too shone when we first set float!"

Swifter and swifter the bright boat sped,
But the hands spake thin like men long dead -
"How striking like that boat were we
In the days, sweet days, when we put to sea.

The ship all black and the ship all white
Met like the meeting of day and night,
Met, and there lay serene dark green
A twilight yard of the sea between.

And the twenty masters of foreign speech
Of every tongue they knew tried each;
Smiling, the silver Captain heard,
But shook his head and said no word.

Then Aflatun and Aristu
Addressed the silver Lord anew,
Speaking their language of Yoonistan
Like countrymen to a countryman.

And "Whence," they cried, "O Sons of Pride,
Sail you the dark eternal tide?
Lie your halls to the South or North,
And who is the King that sent you forth?"

"We live," replied that Lord with a smile,
"A mile beyond the millionth mile.
We know not South and we know not North,
And SULTAN ISKANDER sent us forth."

Said Aristu to Aflatun -
"Surely our King, despondent soon,
Has sent this second ship to find
Unconquered tracts of humankind."

But Aflatun turned round on him
Laughing a bitter laugh and grim.
"Alas," he said, "O Aristu,
A white weak thin old fool are you.

"And does yon silver Ship appear
As she had journeyed twenty year?
And has that silver Captain's face
A mortal or Immortal grace?

"Theirs is the land (as well I know)
Where live the Shapes of Things Below:
Theirs is the country where they keep
The Images men see in Sleep.

"Theirs is the Land beyond the Door,
And theirs the old ideal shore.
They steer our ship: behold our crew
Ideal, and our Captain too.

"And lo! beside that mainmast tree
Two tall and shining forms I see,
And they are what we ought to be,
Yet we are they, and they are we."

He spake, and some young Zephyr stirred
The two ships touched: no sound was heard;
The Black Ship crumbled into air;
Only the Phantom Ship was there.

And a great cry rang round the sky
Of glorious singers sweeping by,
And calm and fair on waves that shone
The Silver Ship sailed on and on.